TABLE OF CONTENTS

INTRODUCTION

Savings, according to Keynesian economics, consists of the amount left over when the cost of a person's consumer expenditure is subtracted from the amount of disposable income he earns in a given period of time. For those who are financially prudent, the amount of money left over after personal expenses have been met can be positive; for those who tend to rely on credit and loans to make ends meet, there is no money left for savings. Savings can be turned into further increased income through investing in different investment vehicles.

Saving is closely related to physical investment, in that the former provides a source of funds for the latter. By not using income to buy consumer goods and services, it is possible for resources to instead be invested by being used to produce fixed capital, such as factories and machinery. Saving can therefore be vital to increase the amount of fixed capital available, which contributes to economic growth.

However, increased saving does not always correspond to increased investment. If savings are stashed in or under a mattress, or otherwise not deposited into a financial intermediary such as a bank, there is no chance for those savings to be recycled as investment by business. This means that saving may increase without increasing investment, possibly causing a short-fall of demand (a pile-up of inventories, a cut-back of production, employment, and income, and thus a recession) rather than to economic growth. In the short term, if saving falls below investment, it can lead to a growth of aggregate demand and an economic boom. In the long term if saving falls below investment it eventually reduces investment and detracts from future growth. Future growth is made possible by foregoing present consumption to increase investment. However savings kept in a mattress amount to an (interest-free) loan to the government or central bank, who can recycle this loan.

MANAGE YOUR PERSONAL FINANCES

It would be nice if you could have one magic formula or one easy trick that made it so you never had to worry about money again. If you are tired of being stressed out about money all of the time, you need to get a hold on your personal finances. There are five keys that can help you get control of your finances. Once you have started following these five steps consistently the stress about your finances should diminish.

• Start with Goals

The first thing you should do is to write specific goals about what you want to do with your life and your money. Finances can affect many different areas of your life. Your goal to travel the world affects how you will plan your finances. Your goal to retire early is dependent on how well you handle your finances now. Home ownership, starting a family, moving or changing careers will all be affected by how you manage your finances. Once you have written down your goals you will need to prioritize them. This makes sure you are paying attention to the ones that are most important to you. You can also list them in the order you want to achieve them, but for a long-term goal like retirement, you should be working towards it while working on your other goals.

- Start by setting long-term goals like getting out of debt, buying a home, or retiring early. These goals can help you focus your shorter term goals.

- Prioritize your goals to help you create your plan (which is the next step).

- Set short-term goals, like following a budget, decreasing your spending, or stop using your credit cards.

• Create a Plan

A plan will help you reach your goals. The plan should have multiple steps. The first part of your plan should be to get control of your budget.

You will need to create a spending plan. The second part of your plan should be to get out of debt. After you have accomplished those two things, you should decide what you want to do with your money to reach your goals. The money you free up from your debt payments can be used to reaching your goals. At this point, you should decide what priorities are the most important to you right now, as long as you are steadily working towards your long-term retirement goals, you can begin to focus on the most important

goals you have set for yourself. Your goals, along with an emergency fund, will help you stop making financial decisions based on fear and help you get control of your situation.

- Your budget is key to success. It is the tool that will give you the most control of your financial future. Your budget can help you reach the rest of your plan.

- Take the time to focus on your budget now. If you need help, consider taking a personal finance class.

• Stick to Your Budget

Your budget is one of the biggest tools that will help you succeed financially. It allows you to create a spending plan so you can focus your money in a way that will help you to reach your goals.

Even after you are out of debt you need to have a budget. It is easy to spend more than you make, and if you stop tracking your spending you can go over and run up debt really quickly. A budget lets you decide how to spend your money. Without the plan, you may spend your money on things that are not important to you, but you want in the moment, and then wonder why you are never reaching the financial milestones you want to set. If you are married you and your spouse need to work together on the budget. This will help you to achieve your goals together and prevent fights.

- Consider switching to an envelope budgeting system that uses cash for the difficult categories.

- Planning ahead can also help you to avoid overspending, which is why budgeting is key to being financially successful.

• Get Out of Debt

Your debt is a huge obstacle to reaching your financial goals. Set up a debt elimination plan that will snowball your payments. While making minimum payments, you focus extra money on one debt at a time and then move all the money you were paying on the first debt to the next debt. Once you are out of debt, you need to make a commitment to stay out of debt. Stop carrying your credit cards around with you, and save up an emergency fund to cover unexpected expenses so you do not need to turn to a credit card to cover them.

- You may want to sell items to find extra money to kick start your debt payment plan.

- A second job can help speed up this process and may be necessary if you want to make lasting changes to your situation.

- Look for areas you can cut in your budget to increase your debt payments too.

• Don't Be Afraid to Ask for Advice

Once you are ready to grow your wealth and begin investing you should speak to a financial planner to help you make your investment decisions. A good advisor will share the risks involved in each investment, and help you find products that match your comfort level while helping you work towards your goals as □uickly as possible. A financial planner can also help you with your budget if you want him to. These types of planners charge an hourly fee, and will help you set up a basic budget if you need the help, and then help you choose investment products when you are ready. Remember that investing is a long-term strategy to building wealth.

A local church or community center may be offering classes on personal finances and budgeting. Occasionally banks and credit unions may do this too.

You can also find a mentor that would be willing to walk you through your budget the first few months. This can help you if you are overwhelmed with your budget. A mentor can also help with other financial areas like opening a business or something similar.

HOW TO START MANAGING YOUR MONEY

How you manage, spend, and invest your money can have a profound impact on your life, yet very few schools teach these important skills. Learning financial savvy can take a while, but the basics are fairly simple and never change. Here's where to get started.

You were probably taught some basic math growing up, but too many people make it all the way to adulthood without ever learning basic money management. Skills like creating a budget, investing for the future, or even how credit cards work are startlingly rare skills. If you're in need of a Money 101, we'll cover the basics for beginners, while also giving you the resources you need to learn more.

The Golden Rules of Personal Finance

Managing your finances feels like nothing but a lot of paperwork and numbers. You make X amount of dollars, you spend Y amount, and you try to make sure Y is less than X. However, your finances are just as much about psychology, habits, and the values you choose to live by. Put another way, your mindset matters just as much as the math.

- Spend less money than you earn: If you earn $30,000/year and you spend $31,000/year, you'll end up in a spiral of debt that's hard to walk away from. If you spend exactly as much as you earn every year, you'll never be prepared for emergencies or major life changes. Spending less than you earn allows you the freedom to save, to prepare for the future, and deal with the inevitable crises that life throws at you. The bigger the gap between your income and your spending, the better.

- Always plan for the future: This doesn't just mean retirement. When a store offers to let you pay off some gadget in 6 months with no interest, you need to know you can pay it off, or avoid that deal. Establishing an emergency fund will allow you to deal with unexpected car repairs or medical bills.

Having a retirement plan will ensure you have income when you're unable to work anymore. Your finances should always look forward beyond the current month.

- Make your money make more money: Want to know how the rich keep getting richer? It's because money can grow while you sleep, provided you save some of it. Properly invested money earns more money over time. Don't just sock all your cash away in a low-interest savings account. Invest in things that will earn you more money than you had before. Sometimes that's an investment account, but sometimes it's starting a business, or even getting an education to get a better paying job.

The most important personal finance rules don't change. What your grandparents did may not work for you. There will always be newer, better tools to manage your money. However, spending less than you earn will always be beneficial. Investing your money will always be better than doing nothing with it. And planning for the future will always be better than blowing your paycheck as soon as you get it.

How to Find a Bank Account

It's neither safe nor advisable to keep all your money under your mattress. You'll need some kind of account to stash your spending money and short-term savings. A bank (or credit union) can hold your money and allow you to access it with an ATM/debit card. Setting up a bank account is easy. You can usually apply online, or go to a branch, ask a teller to open an account, and they'll guide you through the process. Choosing a bank is tougher.

Picking a bank means finding an institution that has the services you need with the fewest fees. Common services include debit cards, ATM access (or at least refunding fees for using other bank's ATMs), paper checks, and a web site where you can see your account balance. While some banks charge monthly fees or require you to have a minimum balance, there are plenty of banks that are worthwhile without either of these requirements. We've discussed more about what to look for in a bank here.

Chances are, most adults in your life have recommendations on which bank they prefer. However, if you can't get a decent suggestion, the FDIC has a tool here that you can use to search for insured banks in your area. The site can find branch locations near you, and give you links to the company's websites where available. Nerd Wallet also has a great online tool here that compares checking accounts from a variety of banks.

Of course, keep in mind that not every bank has physical branches. Some banks like Simple, Ally, or Capital One 360 are online-only. These often come with certain trade-offs (like, you know, not having physical branches), but many offer fewer fees and better services. They also typically offer better interest rates meaning the money you save earns a little extra money just for keeping it in your account than traditional banks, because they don't have as many operating costs associated with physical buildings.

Once you've decided on a bank, either go into a local branch or visit the company's site and ask to open a new account. You'll need to provide basic forms of identification, including your name, social security number, date of birth, and some form of photo ID like a driver's license to prove you are who you say you are. You can check with the bank you want for specifics.

Do you know where your money goes, or does it kind of just disappear from your account? A budget even a basic, barebones one is one of the best ways to make sure you're spending less than you earn, and starting early is important. When you're young and your career is new, you don't have a lot of money. Getting into the habit of categorizing your bills and tracking your expenses will help prevent a lot of financial problems before they start. If you're making a budget for the first time, it may be easier to start with paper, a pen, and a calculator, but we'll get to more advanced tools you can use in a bit.

Start by calculating how much money you make in a month. If you get paid hourly, multiply your wage by the typical number of hours you work each month. Then, write down all of your regular expenses. This includes recurring costs like your rent or mortgage, utilities, car payments, and so on. For more complex things like food, you may need to track what you spend over time. Gather up your receipts for the past few weeks, or use your bank's transaction history if paperwork isn't your thing. If you can't get a precise number, estimate in the meantime. Then, keep track of all your expenses for the next month or two. At the end of each month, add everything up to see how much you're spending in each category.

Ideally, the amount you spend in a month should be lower than the amount you earn. If it's not, start going over your list and see which expenses you can cut down on until it is. If you have to, cut ruthlessly. For some, it may be as easy as cutting those lattes, but for others, you may have some big decisions to make—like whether you can afford to live in that expensive city.

Once you get the hang of tracking your expenses, you can try using a service like Mint to manage it for you. Connect your bank account and it will automatically tag your transactions, so you can easily see how much you're spending on bills, groceries, restaurants, shopping, and other categories. You can also use it to set budgets for different things like groceries or entertainment and get notified when you're going over. You can read more about how to use Mint with our beginner's guide.

So you've gotten into the habit of tracking your spending, and now it's time to create that budget. There are a few different philosophies here. Some people prefer to have a very detailed transaction history with strict allotments for expenses like food, clothing, and entertainment. Others, like financial expert Ramit Sethi, believe that being overly strict doesn't work. Instead, Sethi suggests dividing your money into four categories:

Fixed costs (50-60%): This should include every cost that you know is coming each month, that rarely change. That means rent, gas, power, groceries, your cellphone bill, and anything else that generally stays the same. Some of these may vary a bit from month to month, but are at least somewhat predictable, and are necessary for regular life.

Investments (10%): As you build your savings (which we'll discuss later on), you'll eventually want to invest some of your money so it grows over time. If you have any investments like a company 401(k) that come out of your paycheck, you can count it here.

Savings (5-10%): Short- and long-term savings should go in this category. This includes saving up for vacations, gifts, or large purchases like a new TV or computer. You should also include an emergency fund—which is just a block of money you keep in a savings account for unexpected emergencies like car repairs or sudden bills—in this category.

Guilt-free spending (20-35%): This category is where you can put whatever you want. Dining out, drinking, or splurging on entertainment is often seen as a financial vice, but the truth is, we do these things because we enjoy them. As long as you have the other three categories covered you can spend this money without feeling guilty about your budget.

Those are Sethi's recommendations for young people, but you can (and should) adjust the percentages based on your age, your financial goals, and what you find important. Remember: the more you save, the more money you'll have later on to buy a house, retire early, or achieve other goals. (We'll talk about this more in a bit.)

Ultimately, budgeting just means knowing where your money is going and planning ahead. If you don't want to go to the trouble of writing down every single dime you spend at the gas station, this model will still cover most of what you need to budget for. The only thing you need to decide is how much you'll place in each category. We've included Sethi's recommended percentages as a guide, but you can adjust as needed. If you can't afford to save or invest 10% of your income after expenses, save what you can. You can also add more to your savings rather than forcing yourself to spend

20% of your budget on guilty pleasures. The more you can save, the better!

Getting started with long-term investments will often be one of the hardest parts of your financial life because, when you're just starting out, you don't have much money. For that reason, it's important that you re-examine your investments every time you get a raise or a new job that pays you more. When you make more money, it's tempting to upgrade your life with a new car, apartment, or expensive toys to match your new budget. This is what's called "lifestyle inflation." While it's okay to move up, you'll also never have a better time to boost your long-term savings than when you're already living on a smaller budget than you're earning.

HOW TO SAVE

There are many strategies for saving money each month

• A Newer Method: Pay Yourself First

How It Works

One of the best saving strategies is to pay yourself first. What this means is that you designate a certain amount of your paycheque as your pay (how novel) and you pay that money to yourself before you pay your bills or anyone else. This amount can be $25, $100 or maybe 10% of your pay cheque. It can be any amount that you decide. The important part is that you pay yourself first rather than last. Most people pay all of the bills first and then save anything that might be left over. For most people, that method of saving doesn't really work because nothing is left over to save.

If you pay yourself first, then money will get saved because paying yourself is now your first priority. The nice thing about this method is if your budget is a little tight, it forces you to make adjustments elsewhere and your savings continue to grow.

Paying yourself first also makes sense. Why are you going to work everyday anyway? To earn money for someone else? No way. You go to work to earn money for you and your family. That's why you should pay yourself first—to make sure that your first priority is taken care of: you. It is not likely that anyone else is going to take care of you because they assume that you are taking care of yourself.

• Pay Yourself Automatically

When you pay yourself first, you should set up an automatic way of doing this so that you don't even have to think about it—it just happens. You can get your employer to deduct a certain amount and put it in your RRSP or you can set up automatic transfers with your bank (either online or at your local branch).

Most people who use this method find that they very quickly get use to living on a little less and soon they don't miss the amount that they are paying themselves in their savings account. When you almost forget about automatic savings and let them grow, amazing things happen—automatically. Automatically saving $25 a week turns into $1,300 a year. Now if someone did this over a lifetime, they would get some fantastic results—automatically. If someone automatically saved $100 every paycheque (bi-weekly) from when they were 25 until they were 65, they would end up with almost $415,000 if they only received a 6% rate of interest. Of course someone could afford to save more once they got their house paid off. So their final amount could be much higher. Hopefully you can see how easy it can be to accomplish big things with just a simple automatic setup where you pay yourself first.

• How to Become a Millionaire Automatically

Another amazing thing about using automatic deductions or transfers to pay yourself first is that you can use it to become a millionaire automatically. This may sound crazy, but it actually works. If someone automatically had $200 transferred from each of their bi-weekly paycheques into their investment account from when they were 25 until they were 65, they would end up with over $1,000,000 if they averaged a 7% rate of return on their investments. So a normal person can become a millionaire automatically without winning the lottery. This plan would re□uire a little more sacrifice than most people are willing to make in their twenties, but it is entirely possible.

• The Smartest Method to Save Money: Have a Spending Plan

The very best method to saving money is to create a Spending Plan or a Budget (learn how to make a budget). With a budget you figure out what your income is and what your expenses are. Once you know these two things, you can look for ways to reduce your expenses or increase your income to allocate an amount of money that you can afford to save. This is how the world's largest corporations do it and this is how most of the world's successful business people do it. This method takes a little bit of work at the beginning and a check-up every year or two, but it works.

The secret to this method (if you want to call it that) is to identify what you are spending money on so that you can begin to plan your spending. Once you begin to plan your spending, you will gain control over it and you will be able to plan to spend money on your savings. In other words, you will plan to put money into your savings account. Many people don't like to plan their spending because it involves a little bit of work (once a year). No one is saying that success will come easily, but this little bit of work will pay off big time in many areas of your finances. We dare you to try it - what have you got to lose?

• Ways to Save Money - How to Do It

- A retirement savings account

If this is too much for you, get started by simply putting your money into one savings account, and then grow your savings from there.

You can put money aside on a regular basis for a down payment for a house, a car, or for your retirement. To get started, all of this money can go into one account, and it can double as your emergency fund as long as you don't have "emergencies" on a regular basis.

- Use Many Savings Accounts

If you find a bank or credit union that offers a free savings account, you can open up several savings accounts. Then every time you get paid, you can put money into each of these accounts for every specific thing that you are saving for. This way you can keep your money safe from accidently being spent, and it will be there when you need it.

These accounts don't have to be actual bank or credit union savings accounts, they can be high interest accounts, Tax Free Savings Accounts (TFSAs), RRSPs, term deposits, mutual funds, or other investments. Just make sure that you don't lock up money in a long-term investment that you might need in the short term (learn more about the differences between saving and investing for the short-term versus long-term).

- Under Your Mattress

We hope that you don't do this. Every thief knows that this is the first place to look. Ditto with a roommate. Then there was that guy who dug a hole in his back yard and put $10,000 in cash into a glass jar and buried it. Later when he dug it up, he discovered that the water in the soil surrounding the jar had frozen in the winter and cracked the jar. Water then filled the jar and turned the money into a soupy mess. Because most of the bills were unrecognizable, he was not able to cash most of them in. All he was left with was one broken jar of expensive soup.

- In Your Safety Deposit Box

Lots of people do this—just ask your bank's tellers—they can smell it (old money stinks). Stashing cash in your safety deposit box is definitely safer than using a mattress or burying the money in the back yard, but not much smarter. Money in a safety deposit box does no one any good. It doesn't earn you any interest. The government insures the money you deposit into an account at a bank up to $100,000 (and there are some ways to get higher coverage than this), and if you can't trust the bank with your money, then how can you trust the bank with the stuff in your safety deposit box?

- In Your Bank Account

A cheque account or a regular savings account is no place to save your money. Most of them pay hardly any interest. This is because the bank lends your money to other people when you aren't using it. Money in a regular bank account might get used often, or you might need to withdraw it quickly, so the bank can't lend that money out for very long because you might need it. The bank makes money when they can lend your money out for extended periods of time, and at higher interest rates, so then you earn more interest when they are able to do that.

- High Interest Savings Accounts

These types of savings accounts are usually more restrictive than regular savings accounts, but they pay a lot more interest. Make sure that your bank or credit union is paying you a competitive rate (you can't negotiate but you can move) and then save away. These types of accounts are usually safe, convenient and their interest rates usually move up as bank interest rates move up.

- Other Investments

There are numerous other investments that you can use to save your money: money market funds, bonds, stocks, mutual funds and the list goes on. If you plan to spend the money that you are saving within five years, it is best to find something safe to invest in. For most people a high interest savings account or a term deposit within a Tax Free Savings Account works just fine. These options are safe and sure you know that your money is going to be there when you need it the same can't be said if you choose to invest in something that has a lot more risk. Like the stock market.

• Where to Find Money to Save Each Month

Some things are easier said than done—like saving money. So you want to save money, but where do you find money to save if you don't have anything extra right now? Here are some great places to look: Where to look to find money to save each month.

- Raises at work

When you get a raise, put the extra money you are now earning in the bank. You lived on less before. Do you really need these few extra dollars, or does your savings account need them more?

- Bonuses from work

If you get paid a bonus, bank this money as well. You don't need your bonus for living expenses because it is extra money that you can't count on—that's why it is a "bonus" to your normal wages. Bonuses are perfect for saving. If you need your bonus for living expenses, you probably have other financial challenges that need attention first.

- Overtime pay from work

In some jobs you can volunteer for extra overtime. Consider working a little overtime each week and then treat your overtime pay as something sacred and save it in a special account.

- Extra large commission

If you get paid commission for your job, consider saving a portion of any extra large commission che□ues. It is so easy to blow money and then not know where it went. Use some of your extra large commission cheques to create something you will remember—a nice retirement, a comfortable home, or something else that you would like to save for. Use your savings to create a reward for yourself that will last.

Get It from the Government

- Tax refund

If you get a tax refund, use the money to increase your savings. To find out how to pay less tax so that you can get a tax refund or qualify for a larger refund, speak with your tax advisor or someone you trust. Two ways that many people reduce the amount of tax that they have to pay is by contributing to an RRSP and/or by donating more money to charity. If you set up an automated system where your RRSP or charitable giving is automatically debited from your bank account or deducted from your payche□ue, these options can be easy and affordable.

- Tax Assessment

If property values have fallen significantly in your community, make sure that your tax assessment value is fair. If it's not fair, apply for a re-assessment. In communities where property values have fallen substantially, this can save you a lot of money in property taxes.

- Claim all expenses

If you are self employed, do you do your own taxes or do you have a professional accountant with a professional designation like CA, CGA or CMA do your taxes for you? If your taxes aren't being done by one of these professionals, you could be missing out on some big tax savings. If you think that these kinds of accountants are expensive, that may be true, but it is often more expensive to pay the government thousands of dollars in unnecessary taxes than to pay a good accountant a few hundred dollars to find these savings for you. If you are really thrifty, you can try out the accountant once to see if you are missing any deductions, and then you can go back to your old way of doing taxes and use the tax saving tips that you learned from the accountant.

Find It in Your Expenses

- Look for an expense to cut and save that money

Some people suggest that you increase your savings by cutting back on lattes or ☐uitting smoking, these are good suggestions but there are also other big ways to save money. One way that a lot of people can save money but something they often overlook is to take a serious look at what they spend on their hobbies. Some people spend huge amounts on personal trainers, protein supplements, golf, skiing, and other sports. They don't even consider how much they spend because they believe that they are spending it on something healthy or on something they love. If you have a pressing concern like getting out of debt cutting back what you spend on a hobby, even just for a while, may be a great option to consider.

HABITS LIFESTYLE TO SAVE MORE MONEY

If you're constantly wondering where your money is going, consider how much your daily habits are costing you.

These seemingly small habits, and many more, could be keeping you from saving hundreds, even thousands, of dollars a year.

What habit has saved you the largest amount of money?" and "What are some lifestyle changes that save money? to round up the best and easiest ways people save money every day.

• How to learn the difference between saving a dollar and saving a percentage.

Remember that saving 5% on a $10,000 item is not at all like saving 5% on a $10 item. But in order to process decision problems at different scales, the brain tends to normalize things so the two cases appear similar.

Ever since I studied behavioral economics, I started spending less time worrying about saving 20 cents on spaghetti, but I spent a lot of time thinking about what car to buy and making sure I got a good deal on it. You can buy a lot of spaghetti for a $4k discount on a car, and yet I see people who spend lots of time on grocery coupon clipping but never stop to consider whether they could move to a cheaper apartment, drive a cheaper car, etc."

• Do-it-yourself

I enjoy the challenge of learning new skills and the satisfaction of accomplishing tasks. Among the things I've gotten pretty good at: basic plumbing, interior painting, sewing, bike maintenance, baking, cooking. I'm still working on gardening, and I think I'd like to learn and improve basic construction skills (I'd like to build a deck or patio and repair some fences) and maybe learn about building PCs. Here again, I see it as both entertainment and expense avoidance. Occasionally also exercise.

• Practice delayed gratification.

When you are shopping and your heart leaps at the sight of xyz product, and you think it's love at first sight...WAIT. Save it, bookmark it. Come back to it hours later, then a day later, then days later and gauge, each time, how or whether your level of pumpity-pump" interests stays the same, declines, etc. Never buy on impulse. Sleep on it. Ask yourself: Do you think it'll make you happy a month from its purchase? A few months? A year? Years?

• Do a little math while you shop

Every time I'm out to buy something, I try to figure how much that amount of money would grow to in 5 years at a rate of 10% per year. That comes out to a little more than 60% return.

E.g. if I were to buy something worth $1,000, I'd ask myself: Do I want this thing now, or would I rather have $1,600 in five years?

Depending on what I'm planning to spend the $1,000 on — a guitar with specs that I need or a phone with specs that I don't — I choose to buy or forgo.

"Usually, this approach has resulted in my saving the largest amount of money."

• Don't overspend on status or allure.

Cut back on hanging out with lavish friends who do lavish things you don't really enjoy. If you love skiing, go. But you don't have to go to Aspen during Christmas week and stay at the St. Regis.

Go off-peak, go for fewer days, and stay someplace cheaper maybe with Starwood points. And if you're a real skier, you shouldn't be looking for a hot tub. You should be icing and popping Alleve. And you should be too tired to care about where you're staying except that it's fairly easy to get to the slopes and has a firm, comfortable bed. Stay at a cheap motel. Oh, and go to Alta. Don't go to Aspen."

• Track your spending and set up automatic payments.

Make damned sure that you are doing online banking for every checking and savings account you have, as well as every credit card, loan, and investment. A good resource to tie everything together is Mint.com, which has been mentioned by some others. That is a good option, and will send you free alerts when you get low on funds, as well as give you an idea of your spending trends.

Once you're doing online banking on each of your accounts, set them up to make automatic payments. A lot of banks let you automatically pay bills, both to companies and to individuals. Take advantage of this — it is free and requires almost no effort. With Bank of America, my landlord automatically gets a check from Bill Pay on the 27th of every month, a few days before the 1st, and I never have to even think about rent."

• Prepare your meals ahead of time.

I eat the same lunch nearly every day. Bulk cooking meals is one of the easiest ways to save money, and relieve stress during the week.

In addition to the cost per meal savings that I accumulate over the course of the year I also experience savings in the context of time.

I spend about 2 hours on Sunday preparing my meals. During the week I avoid the stress associated with deciding what I want to eat, and I avoid wasting time waiting in lines or driving to restaurants.

Where I currently work I know that I am billed at $125 an hour to our clients. Even if I only save 15 minutes of time each day (I think I save more relative to my co-workers who eat out), I would be creating an extra $31.25 in potential billable hours.

I aspire to own my own business someday. If at that time I can bill at $125 an hour, and, I maintain my lunch prep which saves 15 minutes every Monday through Friday I will be able to create $7,500 in extra value.

Preparing your lunch every day and not eating out could potentially help you generate $10,000 in savings each year. "It's simple. It's easy. It saves you money."

• Know when to invest in Quality products.

Do NOT skimp on things that you use a lot, especially for productive/creative things or things that help you maintain those capacities (knives, computers, beds, work chairs, gym memberships). Yes, this is a way to save money. Conscious/unconscious workarounds for frequently used important things cost way more in the long run."

• Spend only the money you have.

Listen to your debit card, not your credit card (it lies). I got used to living like I did in college before I was eligible for credit cards — if I didn't have that total amount in my debit card, I couldn't buy it. I keep that mentality today.

Credit cards tempt you and trick you into thinking you have the money when you don't. Before you know it, you're stuck paying back debt, not to mention the horrible interest. Avoid paying any interest on, like, anything. If you already have debt with interest, that is your number 1 priority to get rid of.

• Cut yourself off at midnight.

"Having been a student for the past four year living of a meager income I have set myself a rule to never consume anything other than water after midnight.

This has helped me reduced spending on all useless consumption goods. From alcohol at parties, to snacking at home. In a student life I just cannot see the NEED to ever consume drinks or foods after midnight as that is a time your body is essentially suppose to be asleep.

This strategy doesn't limit your experiences and social life trough college nor does it force you to live extremely frugally, it just reduces useless expenditure."

• Use the '5-Question rule.'

Want or a need? Do I need it? Do I see myself using it? How often? Is it worth the time?

I make it a point to run by these Questions every single time I'm buying something now, given that I earn to pay my rent and food.

Coming from a family in India that is slightly above middle class, I took everything for granted. Bought food I wouldn't eat, clothes I wouldn't wear, art I didn't adore, are some of the many things I splurged my (parents') money on."

• Be happy with what you already have.

Learn to want the things you already have. I'm dead serious. I owned 5 Porsches and 3 Mercedes-Benz (two AMG) before the age of 35. You can count those as the 8 biggest financial mistakes I've ever made and it all had to do with my inability to be content with what I already had. "Believe me, possession of 'things' is a race no one can win.

MONEY MANAGEMENT MISTAKES

While this is great news, unfortunately not saving enough for retirement is still the top vulnerability of most employees. Only 18% know they are on track to reach their income goal in retirement, and the national average savings rate is only about 4%, well below the 10-15% financial planners typically recommend saving for retirement.

Why this the case? It seems one of the biggest problems is that many Americans are still struggling with basic money management. Most employees do not have an emergency fund, 42% are uncomfortable with the amount of debt they have, and 1/3 don't have enough of a handle on their cash flow to spend less than they make each month. It's hard to save adequately for retirement when you're living paycheck to paycheck and struggling with debt.

1. Getting a big tax refund each year.

This is a sign that you may be having too much tax withheld from your paychecks. If this is the only way you're able to save, it's certainly better than nothing (assuming that you actually save that money or use it to pay down debt, of course). The problem is that it's not exactly the most efficient way to save. Not only are you losing the ability to earn anything on that interest-free loan but you also lose access to that money in the event of an emergency. If you tend to get a large refund this IRS calculator can help you determine how to properly fill out your Form W-4. Just be sure to have any extra money in your paycheck set aside in case you do have an emergency. Forced saving is better than no saving at all.

2. Having only a rough idea in your head of where your money goes.

As they say, you can't manage what you don't measure. When I ask someone how much they're spending, they usually list a few bills and other expenses off the top of their head. But once they actually start going through their bank and credit card bills, they're almost always surprised to see where their money is really going. For this reason, you'll want to do the same thing. One option is to go through at least 3 months worth of previous statements and record your expenses by category on an Excel spreadsheet. Both sites also have Apple and Android apps to help you manage your money on the go. Neither approach is necessarily better so just choose the one that you're more likely to actually use.

3. Forgetting those non-monthly expenses.

Some of the largest sources of credit card debt are holidays and vacations. You can easily turn them into monthly expenses by dividing the amount you typically spend each year by 12. You can then have those monthly amounts automatically set aside each month so the money will be there when you need it. While you won't earn a whole lot at today's interest rates, it still beats paying interest on credit card debt.

4. Spending more than you really need to.

Once you know how much you're spending and where your money is really going, think of ways to reduce some of those expenses. After all, regardless of how much you make, don't forget that plenty of people are living on less so you can too. (There are even people who save as much as 75% of their income in order to retire in as little as 5 years.) Do you have subscriptions or memberships that you don't really use? Have you comparison shopped for things like insurance policies, mortgages, cell phone plans, and groceries? Are the purchases you're making for something you really need or just a status symbol? Can you think of lower cost ways of achieving the same result like bringing your own lunch and coffee instead of eating out and stopping at Starbucks on the way to work each day? You may be surprised by how small changes can really add up over time.

5. Paying a little extra on all your credit card debt.

That's certainly better than not making any extra payments or not even paying your bill in full. However, you can pay your debt off faster by putting all the extra money towards the debt with the highest interest rate and making just the minimum payments on the rest. As one balance is paid off, you'd then put those payments towards the remaining card with the highest rate until you're debt free.

6. Thinking that borrowing from your home equity is always a bad idea.

Like most myths, there is some truth in this. After all, you are putting your home on the line so this isn't a good idea if there's a decent chance you won't be able to make the payments. That being said, refinancing high interest credit card debt with a home e□uity loan or line of credit can make sense since your interest rate could be much lower and tax deductible.

7. Thinking that you should never borrow from your retirement plan either.

Like the last one, there certainly is some truth here. Most people think retirement plan loans are free since the interest just goes back into your account. However, there is a very real cost, which is the lost earnings in your account, and a very real risk, which is that any outstanding balance after 60 days of leaving your job could be considered a taxable distribution and subject to a 10% early withdrawal penalty. For those reasons, retirement plan loans should not be taken for frivolous purposes. If you use one to pay off high interest debt, make sure that it's part of a long-term plan to stay debt free. The last thing you want is to run your credit card balance up after depleting your retirement savings.

8. Saving whatever is left at the end of the month.

If you do that, don't be surprised when there isn't anything left to save. Instead, have your savings automatically set aside before you even have a chance to spend it. The easiest way to do that is in your employer's retirement plan since it's deducted right out of your paycheck. The same is true for medical expenses and dependent care if you're eligible for an FSA or HSA. You can also have money automatically transferred from your checking account to savings accounts and an IRA.

9. Contributing just enough to your employer's retirement plan to get the match.

If it's important to know how much to save for holidays and vacations, it's even more important to know how to save for the ultimate holiday/vacation: your retirement. Contributing enough to get your employer's match is a good start but that probably won't be enough. To get an idea of how much you'll need, take a look at your expenses and think about how each one of them might change in retirement to create a retirement budget. For example, your mortgage and other debts may be paid off but you could spend more on travel and health care. Then use a retirement calculator to see how much you need to save. If you can't swing that much, see if your plan has a contribution rate escalator, which slowly increases your contribution rate over time until you hit your goal. After all, it's a lot easier to save 1% more each year then to go from 6% to 15% all at once.

WAYS TO SAVE MONEY WITHOUT MAKING YOURSELF MISERABLE

A budget can be your best friend if you're trying to save your way to a richer life but it can backfire if you don't approach it with the right mindset. One way people get budgeting wrong is by viewing the budget as a means of deprivation instead of as a tool for financial empowerment. Some rebel and go off on a spending binge to release those feelings of frustration. A budget is your ticket to financial freedom. If the thought of living on a budget has you down in the dumps, here are some tips for keeping your eye on the savings prize.

1. Automate your savings

Building up a savings habit or any habit for that matter takes time and practice. Automation can make the adjustment a little less painful. Set up recurring transfers from your checking account to your savings account. It's is one of the best ways to save money when you're brand-new to it. By moving the money automatically, you have to work harder to get your hands on it for spending purposes.

2. Start small

Goal-setting is a good way to keep yourself motivated to save but only if your goals are realistic. If you decide that you want to save $10,000 in a year when you've never had so much as $20 in a savings account before, you're setting yourself up for a big disappointment. Start with smaller goals—say, socking away $25 a week til you hit your first $500—so that your goal is achievable. Then you can celebrate victory and up the ante when you reach your target.

3. Look for ways to beef up your income

Money to save comes by two roads: spend less, or earn more. If you've trimmed down your spending but you're still not saving as fast as you'd like, earning more may be the answer. We don't have a secret formula for how to make a lot of money but we do have some pointers for maxing out your paycheck. Taking on more hours at your current job is one option. Asking for a raise is another. If you can't do either, consider getting a part-time gig or starting a side hustle. Could you drive for Lyft or Uber? All of these can lead to a boost in income, which could boost your savings in turn.

SAVING TIPS

Some of the best ways to save money are strategies people often overlook. If you've made up a budget but you're still looking for extra dollars and cents, take a look at these helpful saving money tips.

Pay in cash. Debit and credit cards are convenient but studies show that we spend more when we swipe plastic versus handing over paper money.

Collect your loose change daily. Once you make the switch to cash, set up a jar for any loose change that ends up in your pocket or purse each day. All those pennies, nickels, dimes and quarters can add up to more savings faster than you might think.

Eliminate grey charges. Grey charges are small fees that can drain your savings potential in a big way. Go the extra distance to your own bank's ATM and avoid paying a fee to withdraw cash. Dump recurring subscriptions that you don't use.

Become a coupon clipper. You don't have to become an extreme couponer to score big savings at the grocery store or the mall. Use an app like Retail Me Not or Coupons.com to snag money-saving coupons the moment you need them, right on your smartphone.

Take advantage of student or employer discounts. If you're in school (at any age), your student ID can save you money at movie theaters, restaurants and more. If you're working, check to see if your job offers any discounts on things like fitness or entertainment. Just be sure to only research purchases you were already planning to make. You'll diminish your ability to save if you buy something just because it's a great deal.

Pack your own lunch. Eating out can destroy your efforts to save, especially if you're doing it every day. Packing your own lunch keeps more money in your wallet and it can be healthier to boot.

Switch banks to avoid costly fees. Overdraft fees and monthly maintenance fees can eat your savings alive if you let them. Move to a credit union or an online bank to eliminate expensive fees.

Raise your deductibles. Set your insurance deductibles higher. It means you'll pay more out of pocket if you need to file a claim but most of us will save money in the long run anyway.

Adjust your thermostat. Turn your thermostat up in the summer and let your place stay a little cooler in winter. You'll shave big bucks off your utility bills each month.

Take care of your wheels and yourself. Keep up with basic car maintenance and preventative care like dental checkups. If you and your car are both in good working order, you're a lot less likely to have to spend money on unexpected health emergencies or car repairs.

SAVING FOR THE FUTURE WHILE ENJOYING

The desire to prepare for the future and save versus the impulse to live for the present and enjoy earnings now. People know that nobody is promised tomorrow, but they also don't want to live out their retirement years with limited choices, or none at all.

So how can people strike a successful balance between these seemingly competing desires? Based on my work with financial planning clients, here's my five-step plan:

Understand your cash flow. I'm going to make a bold statement here: Nothing will affect your financial future more than your ability to understand your household cash flow. If you want more money to save for the future or to spend now, you have to understand your current spending patterns and habits to get there. Check in on your spending weekly; that takes far less time than a monthly review, and it's easier to catch places you may have spent more than you planned. It's easy to live lean for a week if you've overspent in a previous week. It's a lot harder to catch up if you've been overspending for a month.

Learn to say "no" by deciding on your "yes." The clearer you are about what you want to do in the short and long term, the easier it is to make spending choices that you'll be happy with when you look back at them. Before I married the woman who became my wife, I used to feel deprived if we weren't going out to eat often. On our honeymoon, I discovered that what I really wanted to do was to travel the world with her. Once that became the big yes, I wasn't depriving myself if I didn't go out to eat. If I did go out to eat, I was depriving myself of what I really wanted, which was to travel more. That single idea helped me change my habits entirely and build up the money we needed to take a big trip every year.

Limit your monthly bills. Eric Kies talks about Money Past, Money Present, and Money Future in his First Step Cash Management system. Money Past is all of the money you've agreed to spend at the beginning of the month — things like rent, utilities, and student loan payments. While buying a new car may not seem like a big deal if you think you can afford it, adding on a car loan to your Money Past comes with a major tradeoff: It limits your day-to-day spending (Money Present), and it cuts into your ability to save for the future as well (your Money Future). Be careful; I regularly see young couples adding to their Money Past bucket, limiting their present and future spending choices.

Automate your savings for present and future goals.
Chances are you get paid by direct deposit, and it's easy to direct funds into multiple accounts. Beyond your basic emergency fund, I've seen clients have a lot of success in setting up multiple savings accounts to have balances grow for specific goals (a trip to Europe, for example, or a new car). This allows you to see the specific progress you're making. The same concept applies for retirement plans at work. If you can save that money automatically before it reaches your bank account, you're far more likely to continue saving those funds in the future and even to increase your contributions over time.

Plan for spontaneity. This may sound contradictory, but I think it's essential. Many people I've spoken to resist tracking their spending because it feels constraining. A good solution to this is to build in money that is purely for spontaneous spending. If you know there's money in your budget that is there for the sole purpose of spending it, it protects the money that you're saving into other accounts by providing an outlet for a spur-of-the-moment decision.

INCONCLUSION

Education system teaches us every thing but it never teaches us how to manage money properly. We are educated and skillful but we are still unaware about the fact that how to utilize our financial resources and do lots of major and minor mistakes in our real life. We all are aware about the financial crisis which is currently faced by the whole world. Considering all the above aspects facts about how to utilize your financial resources properly

The easiest way to get your savings working for you is to set things up so that you automatically add a little bit each month to your savings.

Manage your money and enjoy the freedom that comes with it! Today that may be a new thought or an oxymoron you never wanted to entertain. With Canadians spending more than 20 % above their incomes, chances are you are among those who need to reassess your financial picture.

Many couples live with large amounts of stress because of the uncertainty of where they actually stand financially. Today you can begin to end this stress and take control of your finances.

The following is an eye opener for couples who have never seen on paper or their computer screen the amount of money that comes in to their home and how it is spent. This realization alone has caused couples to change their spending habits. Others have realized that their spending habits are increased around stress and have taken aim at lowering their stress

Investing is an overwhelming area of finance, so start small and learn what you can.